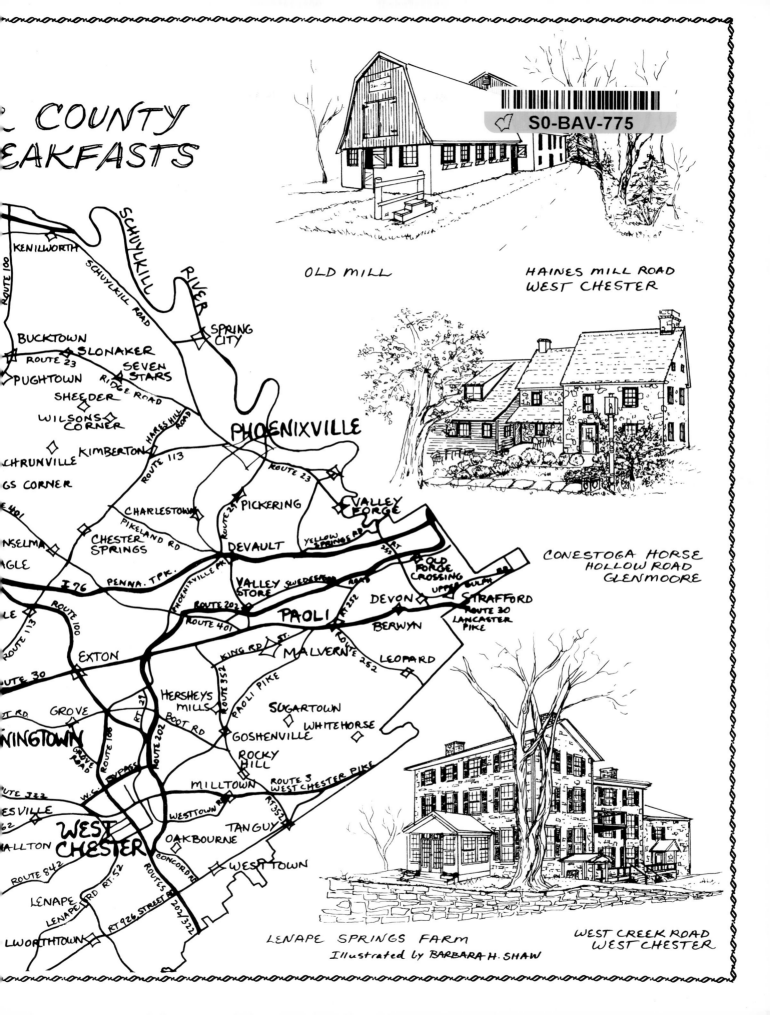

COUNTY
EAKFASTS

OLD MILL

HAINES MILL ROAD
WEST CHESTER

CONESTOGA HORSE
HOLLOW ROAD
GLENMOORE

LENAPE SPRINGS FARM
Illustrated by BARBARA H. SHAW

WEST CREEK ROAD
WEST CHESTER

THE FOUR SEASONS OF CHESTER COUNTY
VOL. III

*Todays Temporary and I
want to wish you
a wonderful New Year!
Jan. 1994*

ABOUT THE COVER

Ah, the exhilaration of a carriage ride through Chester County country in the early spring, perhaps en route to a bed and breakfast inn.

The Four Seasons
Red Hamer

*This Volume features some
of the charmingly beautiful bed and breakfast
homes of Chester County with emphasis on
landscapes and period architecture*

*Published and Distributed by
Four Seasons Book Publishers
Red Hamer, Owner-President
P. O. Box 0222
West Chester, PA 19380*

# of Chester County   Volume III

Author and Photographer

FAIRMAN ROGERS Memorial Carriage Ride arrives at Owen J. Roberts estate, Chester Springs, May, 1989. Carriages (left to right) — Dr. Donald Rosato, Chester Springs; Dr. Clarkson (Bud) Addis, Birchrunville; John Landan, Chester Springs

First Printing — 6,000 Copies — November, 1992

ISBN Number 0-9605400-7-5

Printed By
Taylor Publishing Company
Dallas, Texas

This book is dedicated
To Rose Marie (Ranée) Collins
My sister, my artist, my friend.
Oct. 31, 1928 — June 26, 1992

Contents   Page

A Dog's Day In The Country

The Greeks explained happiness as "the full use of your powers along lines of excellence." John F. Kennedy drew on that assessment at an Oct. 31, 1963 press conference, explaining why he enjoyed the presidency. It was less than a month before his assassination.

His statement pretty much sums up my personal fulfillment in photographing the highways, byways and architecture of Chester County. It is a county resplendent in creative restoration and an ongoing challenge to meet that excellence, to do it all justice.

I have heard the concern for over-crowding and the "paving over" of Chester County. Yet, BECAUSE OF the skill of some of our fine builders and landscape artists, this county no doubt is far more beautiful than it ever was. After all, they didn't have gas driven lawn mowers, rototillers, etc. way back when. And most of those old pictures show it!

Just drive through the neat little towns of Font, Embreeville, Unionville, Landenberg or Guthriesville, etc., and witness the respect for history in street after street in West Chester; or the ongoing revival on Bridge Street in downtown Phoenixville. Downingtown's East Lancaster Avenue has one restored architectural relic after another named after its original owner, and dated on small signs.

• • •

I attempted to display the wide variety of architecture by photographing about one third (20) of the growing number of bed and breakfast establishments. There is a high mortality among these inns so by the time the next book emerges more will have come and some will have gone.

An exhilarating method of seeing the open countryside is by carriage, and for the second straight book I have featured this elegant sport. All of these carriage photographs were to have appeared in a previously planned volume called: "20 Days of Elegance," featuring carriage meets on the East Coast. But, alas, I had 18 rolls of film together with a camera bag and lens stolen at a Newport, R.I. carriage competition in 1989. So some of that work is featured here by default.

Of course, there are always setbacks in creating a book, particularly when they are developed over a period of time. This book required four years and was developed out of 3500 photographs, some of which will be used in *THE FOUR SEASONS OF CHESTER COUNTY VOL. IV*. The devastating blow in making this volume was the loss of my sister, my artist, my friend, Ronnie, to ovarian cancer on June 26, 1992.

Ron had appeared with me at the initial book signing for Vol. II in 1988 at the Chester County Historical Society. She had illustrated the covered bridges and the northern and southern Chester County maps in pen and ink on the end pages of that book. The work was exquisite.

A former teacher of art, she also illustrated a marvelous variety of dogs for my daughter Lynne Hamer's book, *NAME THAT DOG* which was published in 1990.

• • •

Ron had already begun work on the maps for Vol. III. And she was looking forward to drawing the beautiful homes that make up the bed and breakfast section; especially, the dwarfed burro "Toy" who posed in front of The Bankhouse. But, alas, she became too weak to continue. "There never is enough time," she said.

My former wife, Barbara Shaw, took the paint brush like a baton and ran with it. Barbara, who illustrated my first three books, flew to Maine and brought off her best work yet. Must have been the Wyeth air!

Although I had plenty of comrades in arms — Judy and Dr. Don Rosato of Chester Springs, who set up ALL of the carriage pictures, and dozens of others who helped me to dig up one historical nugget after another — the business would have been lonely were it not for SHAMROCK, my constant and always loyal companion. Shammie, a part Labrador and part Golden Retriever, is shown below looking out on a lovely farm house tucked into an East Bradford hillside at Valley Creek and Conner Roads. I always knew it was the right picture to take when Shammie's fur went up.

— RED HAMER.

SPRING • SUMMER

DAFFODIL HISTORY — William Penn's daughter Laetitia sold the property (page 6 and above) to the Gregg family and in 1732 the left portion of the house was built, making it one of the oldest in Kennett Township. It lies between Chandlers Mill and Bucktoe Roads. That's the Bucktoe Creek (left).

Daffodils on the hill were marketed in Wilmington by the Harker family in the 1950s. Present owners Margaretta and Tom Brokaw (not the TV anchor) built the wooden portion of the house (inset) set off by the 250-year-old sycamore tree. General Howe led his troops through the area to the Battle of the Brandywine in 1775.

COMING . . . AND GOING — Striking carriage of Louisa Plummer, Telegraph Road, West Chester, strikes out on the first leg of the Fairman Rogers Memorial Drive, May, 1989, down a hill and along a stream of the Bryn Coed Farm, (left) and through the woods (above). Seventeen carriages took part in the March of Dimes, Delaware Valley Chapter, event.

JACK RUSSELL straining at her owner's leash marked the site of t[he] gathering of the carriages for the start of the Fairman Rogers Drive. The si[te] is the Bryn Coed Farm, Chester Springs. Drive then moved on to Charl[es] Grace's Owen J. Roberts estate (below). Rear patio overlooks the pond.

CROSSING THE BRIDGE to the Drive's next stop, the Birchrunville Store, is the Robinson carriage of Crebilly Farm, West Chester. Jack Fairclough of Newton, N.J. parks in front while a couple enjoys a cocktail on the rear deck of the store.

RED WHEELS AND YELLOW WHEELS — The carriages roll onto the Owen J. Roberts Estate in the Spring of '89 for the second stop of the Fairman Rogers Memorial Drive as laughing children greet guests with flowers. The coaches: James K. Robinson, Crebilly Farm, West Chester (left); Ms. Louisa Plummer (middle); and Ms. Linda Buzzard (bottom).

ON TO PHILADELPHIA the next day as G. Mason Cadwell, of Unionville, leads the parade from City Hall (John Landan, Chester Springs, follows) to the Philadelphia Museum of Art (right). Fairman Rogers (1833-1900) was America's foremost authority on four-in-hand driving and the charity event was held in the prominent Philadelphian's memory.

THE HATS HAVE IT at the Radnor Races, 1989 edition, as the ladies (from three years to ?) flaunt their plumage and wide brims in a spring event that has taken on an increasingly gala character. Yes, there are horse races on the flat and over the brush. But the antique car and carriage parades and tailgating from (in this case) a Rolls Royce lend an unmistakable elegance.

UNDER THE MULBERRY TREE — The 10,000 or so race goers at the 1992 Winterthur Point to Point were shielded by distance and a hill from seeing this beautiful sight. Above, a tip of the fedora and the driver's whip to a lovely lady along the tail of the carriage parade.

SNUG HOLLOW FARM — in a county where historical homes are measured by the number of times they are listed on tours, this property at 1160 N. New St., West Chester, is among the desirable. Its main section built in the early 1800s, the house fell into disrepair and was occupied by squatters in the 1930s. When Bill Breuniger bought it in 1951, it consisted of four walls, a roof and a stone foundation. Since then it has been opened twice for Chester County Day and twice for the West Chester Holiday tour. It has a country store in the basement, not for selling items, but for displaying collectibles.

From The
DEVON
HORSE
SHOW

PRACTICE MAKES PERFECT for four-in-hands at the Devon Horse Show, 1989 variety. Robert Weaver, Peoria, Illinois, Grand Champion many times, takes his team through the preliminary competition at Blackburn Farm, Berwyn (top), later makes the four-mile "pleasure drive" to the stadium (middle) where he makes his entry. Carriages of the one-horse (left) and two-horse variety step through their paces at the farm before entering the main ring.

To A Country Wedding

BRAD DYER SWEEPS Anne Theurkauf off her feet literally as they celebrate their 1991 marriage in this idylic setting in Chester Springs. It happens to be the colonial Lone Pine Farm on Elbow Lane where the bride was raised by her parents, Dr. Edward and Patricia Theurkauf. The fully catered and orchestrated affair raised the roof on several tents.

BUCOLIC GETAWAYS — Happy Days Farm (above), located on Route 113 near Eagle, was to become the site of a large mall sometime after 1992. The Nantmeal Road pastoral scene (right) together with 200-year old stone structures, was too far out of the way to become a mall, but don't hold your breath.

MERESTONE — You can't get much further south in Chester County than this. State of Delaware line runs through the middle of Merestone farm house (above). The other part is in London Britain Township. Overlooking the White Clay Creek, the picturesque barn and farm house helped to establish the township in 1725. This piece of history is located on Watson's Mill Road near Landenberg.

SOMETHING OLD, SOMETHING NEW. . .and definitely esthetic. David Townsend House (right), built in 1785 and located at 225 N. Matlack St., West Chester, was on the Walking Tour in 1992. Named after botanist, banker, civic leader and humanitarian (1787-1858). Noted architect Henry Price constructed in 1931 a mix of colonial and federal complete with ionic columns into beautiful home above at E. Virginia and N. Matlack St. Price introduced elements of colonial Philadelphia waterfront homes razed in 1920.

BED And BREAKFAST SECTION

MAGGIE THE CAT (right photo and page 23) and lambs overlook their Campbell House bed and breakfast domain on Doe Run Road near Unionville. Farmer and Quaker William Windle built oldest section of house in 1746, crowded by seven children. Left side was built in 1794.

PHEASANT HOLLOW FARM B&B in West Bradford Township is a post and beam country house built on the site of an earlier farmhouse using the original stone reflected in the 200-year old spring house (right). Ambiance is fireplace cozy, early American set in wooded seclusion. For reservations, call Bob and Barbara Adams at 215-384-4694.

CORNERSTONE — The father of our country was not even born yet when this mother of all Chester County bed and breakfast estates became in 1704 part of a land grant from William Penn of England to William Penn's son in Philadelphia. Original kitchen constructed in early 1700s is marked by the light faced stone (left). Cornerstone, located at Buttonwood and Newark Rds., Landenberg, was completed in 1820 and turned into a B&B in 1979 by Linda Chamberlin and Marty Mulligan. The elegant living room (above) is adorned with 18th century pieces and two fireplaces, the mantels of which were hewn by Hessian soldiers after the Revolutionary War. Golden Retriever Ben graces front of the fieldstone estate.

CORNERSTONE's renovated stone barn (above) graced by hostess Linda Chamberlin and retrievers Mitzy and Ben, is the home of two furnished guest apartments.

JAKE THE CAT finds canopied Chinese wedding bed to her liking. Hallway shows off more antiques. Full sized swimming pool and riding bikes are outdoor offerings. For reservation call 215-274-2143.

LANDENBERG LANDMARK — The Wool House (above) was the sorting and washing shed for the wool mill which made Landenberg a boom town of 1300 people in the last 25 years of the 19th century. The original part of the picturesque structure was built about 1780. The Landenberg Hotel and General Store first opened in 1872 and were the social center of town with a dance floor on the second level of the store. That since burned and the town itself "died" in the early 20th century. The Wool House had four apartment units in 1992.

HIGHLAND FARM B&B

HIGHLAND FARM, an 1850 Georgian Revival House set in autumn splendor high atop a hill near Rt. 162, was the boyhood home of pioneer family historian Gilbert Cope. The Hoopes family then lived there for 90 years and was known all over the U.S. for its Arabian horses. Attorney John O'Brien and wife Shirley (above) bought it in 1985 and turned it into a charming B & B with a view from its pool as far as the eye can see. For reservations call 215-431-7026.

WALNUT HILL B&B

WO SEASONS of Walnut Hill B&B along Chandlers Mill Road, vondale. White tail deer find the bucolic setting a perfect place to mp along Red Clay Creek. Host Tom Mills poses with yellow Lab "Devonshire Cream" about where Chandlers' grist mill and cider mill once stood. With wife, Sandy, Tom helps maintain charm of circa 1840 guest home. For reservations, 215-444-3703.

LIGHTED HOLLY Bed and Breakfast, so named because the holly tree is lit most of the year at the 216 N. Union street residence in Kennett Square. Built between 1820 and 1840, the architecture is Federal style colonial. Most B&Bs have at least one fireplace bedroom and that is true of innkeeper Carolyn Zinner's home. Her busy times are spring and fall. For reservations, call 215-444-9246.

ROBERT SCARLETT built this American Four Square house at the corner of Garfield and W. State St., Kennett Square, in 1910 and innkeeper Sue Ascosi turned it into a bed and breakfast in 1990. Scarlett's son, George, who lived next door, was a state senator. The benches (right) are a reflection of the Scarlett Quaker heritage. For reservations call 215-444-9592.

A COLLECTION OF 200 SANTA CLAUS DOLLS was a main attraction in 1991 when Meadow Spring Farm (circa 1836) was opened to the West Chester Historical Society Tour. The 130 acre farm, which can house up to 12 guests, is located on Rt. 926 near Longwood Gardens. Cows, pigs, lambs and horses dot the farm with outdoor pool and indoor jacuzzi, pool table, ping pong. Anne Hicks and daughter Debbie Axelrod won Preferred Host Quarterly Award by *B&B Times Magazine*, 1987. For reservations, call 215-444-3907.

CONESTOGA HORSE B&B

IN A STILL OF THE NIGHT — That cottage (below) was called a butcher shop during Prohibition. "It turned out there was a still in the attic," said Mrs. Richard Moore, who runs the Conestoga Horse Bed and Breakfast out of the main house (left). "The people that lived there were from Europe. They were used to making their own. They would have a big party here every Sunday. People would come all the way from Philadelphia. The FBI raided the place and Hollow Road became known for that." The Moores at one time owned all of the land at that corner of Rt. 401 and Hollow Road in East Nantmeal, then sold it to Journey's End Farm, retaining the main house (circa 1760) and the cottage (probably older). Richard Moore built the barn complex for Journey's End (Page 39), located about two miles west of Ludwigs Corner. The horse boarding farm has produced a national pony champion, Amanda Forte, daughter of Journeys End owners Gary and Elizabeth Forte.

FAUNBROOK, circa 1860, located where Rosedale Ave. meets Lenape Road in West Chester, is a beauty in all seasons thanks to its Italian Federal design. Six generations of the Darlington family grew up in Pomona Hill (c. 1761) across the street (left insert) and the Darlington family is a big part of the Faunbrook legend. Named after a half-goat, half-man weathervane and Goose Creek that rambles through the property, Faunbrook came alive under Smedley Darlington who bought the place in 1867. "Uncle Smedley" jumped in with both feet when the oil fever hit. When that fever ebbed, he invested in western land. His personal wealth rose to an estimated $1 million. He established two banking houses, founded the Chester County Republican Party and served two terms as a U.S. Congressman. In 1887 he introduced his six daughters to Washington society and "lived a lavish lifestyle" as the *Philadelphia Sunday Times* put it. West Chester already knew that. Every year he would hire a trolley to bring in friends to his annual Fourth of July fireworks party. In 1897 the country went bust and he lost most of his fortune.

Isabel Darlington lived at Faunbrook in 1940 when the first Chester County Day tour went through. She became the first female lawyer in Pennsylvania and the first female president of the Chester County Bar Assn. Her exchange of plants with the duPonts at Longwood Gardens is reflected in the flower displays in these photographs. Judy and John Cummings bought the place from the Darlington family in 1982 and turned it into an elegant bed and breakfast with an emphasis on weddings. Ashley Smiley, of Glenmoore, is our prospective bride model who poses (from left) at the entrance with "Shamrock," in the sitting room, in the foyer with a Harry Dunn art display and reflected in the living room mirror. For reservations, call (215) 436-5788.

DUCK HILL FARM B&B

DUCK HILL FARM — Pick your own fru
from the apple-pear orchards or strawberr
raspberry vines of this handsome stone coloni
estate (circa 1750) nestled in the wooded hi
north of Guthriesville off Rt. 322 on Litt
Washington-Lyndell Road. Spend a night in t
converted ice house complete with firepla
(above and above right) or in the main hou
(left and upper left). Pritikin Diet people spe
three months here as John and Marie Reid
first guests in 1983. They enjoyed the spring f
pool after a day of shooting a movie at the
center in Downingtown, and the fact that the
pets were welcome. Featured in the *New Yo
Daily News* in 1987. For reservations, (21
942-3029.

CLUTCH OF SPRING GOSLINS with M
and Pa Canada geese (right) at nearby Templ
Road farm and pond.

FRANKLIN HOUSE B&B — Mary Ann Porter has been running her bed and breakfast (left) at 339 N. Franklin St., West Chester, since she joined the national Bed and Breakfast League in 1980. The lovely Federal style three-story dates to 1856 and lists Gibbons G. Cornwell, burgess of West Chester (1950-53), among those who grew up here. "There are two BB holes in one window. His brother is responsible for that," declared Mrs. Porter. The house has twice been on the Chester County Day tour. For reservations, (215) 696-1665.

HEDGEROW B&B (right), located in Chadds Ford on Rt. 52, offers special occasion services. Innkeepers Barb and John Haedrich will select a cake for a birthday or anniversary if notified in advance. Rooms are located in a post and beam carriage house in back of the Victorian home. For reservations, (215) 388-6080.

LOG HOUSE B&B (below), on Rt. 10 three miles west of Oxford, has indoor activities in barn; hiking, biking and picnicing, and a great view of the Amish buggies on Rt. 10. For reservations, call Arlene Hershey at (215) 932-9257.

FOX QUARRY B&B — Constructed in the shadow of his father's Red Willow Farm house which dates to 1710 (stucco over logs with short 6'10" high ceilings), beautiful Fox Quarry has been an inn to folks from "all over the world for eight years," according to innkeepers Tom and Barb Simpers. Located on Walnut St., just off Rt. 926 near Willowdale, expansive stone back patio features pond with several varieties of fish. For reservations, (215) 444-1486.

BANKHOUSE B&B — Neighbor's miniature donkey "Toy" mugs for camera agai[n] backdrop of innkeeper Diana Bové's circa 1765 roadhouse at 875 Hillsdale Rd., W[.] Chester. "I love to feed people," said Diana, who apprenticed at a New England B&B. [For] reservations, (215) 344-7388.

LENAPE SPRINGS FARM B&B — The Brandywine Picnic Park along the Brandywi[ne] Creek (left) is right up W. Creek Rd. from this stunning farm B&B run by Sharon and B[ob] Currie. They board horses, raise beef and provide four rooms for guests. A building behi[nd] the big house dates to 1728, "but the Revolutionary War went around us," said Sharon. [For] reservations, (215) 793-2266.

THE HILL HOUSE B&B — Atop a precipice overlooking Rt. 100 and the Brandywine in Chadds Ford; an historic home built in 1770 which was penetrated by a cannonball during the Revolutionary War. English breakfast and afternoon tea served by its very English innkeeper Penny Farley, a native of Essex, England, seen on her porch admiring the March onion snow. A bird at her feeder (right). For reservations, (215) 388-1596.

LD MILL B&B — The entrance is at the other ..e of this barn attached to 1710 converted grist ..ll at 680 Haines Mill Rd., a West Chester ..dress but only two miles from Longwood Gar-..ns. Innkeeper Sally Flynn has run the rustic B&B ..ce 1983 — between fox hunts with the Bran-..wine Hunt. She rides where the British marched ..ring the Revolutionary War — along the Pocop-.. Creek. For reservations, (215) 793-1633.

PILLARIED — Greek Revivalist Thomas U. Walter designed this former Rothrock Estate at 300 W. Miner St. In 1961 new owner George Watson replaced the columns with larger ones. Watson found a mansion being torn down in South Carolina, bought the pillars for $300., had them delivered for $46, and installed them just after he and Louise were married. Daily Local News columnist Bill Hauck called Watsons "the Scarlett O'Hara and Rhett Butler of West Chester."

AUTUMN

EVERHART PARK along western edge of West Chester is never lovelier than in the fall. Land was left to borough by Benjamin Everhart in 1904, last surviving member of a family that, in the 19th century, constructed over 300 brick buildings in the borough and produced a physician, a nationally known botanist and a congressman.

BEHIND THE YELLOW WHEEL of Dr. Clarkson (Bud) Addis' carriage goes a timber race at the 1990 Pennsylvania Hunt Cup, Unionville, while more carriages, the Chester County Tour Antique Car Club and esthetic picnics (left page) are very much a part of the side show. That 1967 Lincoln truck lid made a great table.

A LOVELY AUTUMN WEDDIN[G] took place this November day in 1991 [at] beautiful Springton Manor in Glenmoo[re.]

The farm grounds provided an into[x]icating strolling area for the guests. T[he] wedding took place in the Manor Hou[se] (upper right) which dates to 1833. It w[as] the center of life on the farm owned th[en] by Congressman Abraham McIlvain[.] The 300 acres were set aside by Willia[m] Penn in the 1700s for his own use. T[he] entire site is listed on the National Re[g]ister of Historic Places. The Chest[er] County Parks and Recreation Departme[nt] runs it as a demonstration farm. T[he] Manor House is available for private pa[r]ties and public functions.

The black goose belongs to a neighbor.

SPRINGTON MANOR FARM

52

MAIN LINE CONNECTION — Morstein Station (c. 1870s), first named Woodland and then Zermatt Station, was built to serve local villagers. Porch and two-story frame addition were added in late 1880s. Located on King Road west of Malvern, the Penna. RR station ceased operation and sold the property to Roy Weston, founder of the environmental management company, in 1969. Weston permitted the last station master, Clair Gunkle, to live there until his death in 1980. Weston restored the station in 1986-88 which houses his auditors.

LUDWIGS CORNER — Intersection of Rt. 100 and 401 is the gateway to the northwest corner of Chester County and to the Ludwigs Corner Horse Show the second weekend in September.

LENGELLY FARM (top of page) is one of the oldest homes in oneybrook. One corner was built in 35. There were two houses and they re joined in 1834. Located at 603 estnut Tree Road, grounds sport an cient springhouse (left) and beau-ul antiques on the inside belonging Grier and Nancy Saunders.

UTHRIESVILLE ROAD OUSE (above) is all set for Hal-ween along Rt. 322, while Down-gtown's famous log cabin built in 10 (right) stands immortal near the nks of the Brandywine. Cabin is of edish log construction and was later ned by Thomas Downing who set-d there in 1735 and after whom owningtown was named.

FARM CITY TOUR came to the Willisbrook Farm (above) on Sugartown Road, Willistown Township, in 1991. It was one of four farms opened to show how they are run. Hay rides and pumpkin picking were the main events.

LUCKY HILL FARM — More than 50 years after the left side of this farm house (right) was built in 1721, the British came marching down Lucky Hill Road from Marshalton. It was then known as the Bon Farm after the original owner. The farm house has a walk-in fireplace and a "welcome window." If you wanted guests, you put a lighted candle in the window. Obviously, the candle was not lit when the British came walking by. The right side of the house was built in 1762, and the Normandy barn in 1801, according to a three by four foot date stone in the form of a sea shell on the west end. The much photographed and painted residence, occupied in 1992 by Lydia Bartholomew, was the featured home in an edition of *Pennsylvania House* magazine.

CANNERY ROAD AND RT. 162 in Embreeville along the west branch of the Brandywine is one of the most scenic autumnal locations in Chester County. The residence (above) was built about 1850. The completely restored building below, cupola added, was never a schoolhouse, as it appears, only a store, then a residence, and empty in 1992. That's the Embreeville Bridge to the left and the Embreeville feed mill to the left of that.

Valley Forge

A PLACE FOR GENERALS, horses and deer (upper left hand corner) — Four generals were housed at Valley Forge during the Revolutionary conflict; General Henry Knox behind the horse (upper right), General Maxwell (left) and Major General Lord Stirling (right) whose aide de camp was Major James Monroe, fifth president of the U.S. The Federal style house with the blue shutters (above) was home to two deer at the side of its garage on this November day.

MALVERN PREP
CAMPUS

A DAY IN NOVEMBER, 1991.

STILL BLUE WATERS and orange berries provide
the accent colors for a gray East Goshen barn.

THAT'S ALL ONE HOUSE on the other side of the woodpile, maybe the longest in Chester County, certainly in the picturesque village of Lyndell. The name of the place is ACREY.

THE BIGGEST ATTRACTION in Lyndell, however, is the Lyndell General Store, built in 1817 along the banks of the east branch of the Brandywine Creek. The post office went into operation in 1890. Proprietor John Speakman just finished adding a tackle and bait shop on the near side. The store is on Rt. 282 south of Glenmoore and the Marsh Creek Lake.

IN CHESTER COUNTY, OLD IS BEAUTIFUL. . .and so is this farm house along Rt. 82 enroute to Honeybrook. Deep window sills, random width floors and a walk-in fireplace are features of Springhill Farm, circa 1780.

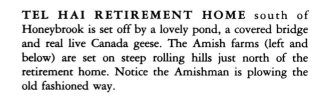

TEL HAI RETIREMENT HOME south of Honeybrook is set off by a lovely pond, a covered bridge and real live Canada geese. The Amish farms (left and below) are set on steep rolling hills just north of the retirement home. Notice the Amishman is plowing the old fashioned way.

WALLACE TOWNSHIP
MUNICIPAL BUILDING

BUILT IN 1810 AS THE INDIANTOWN SCHOOL
FOR SPRINGTON MANOR

REBUILT IN 1859 AS A SCHOOL AND
COMMUNITY CENTER

DEDICATED MAY 23, 1991
BY
WISSAHICKON CHAPTER NATIONAL SOCIETY
DAUGHTERS OF THE AMERICAN COLONISTS

SITTING HIGH ON A HILL overlooking the western Chester County town of Glenmoore is the historic Wallace Township building.

THE OLD GRIST MILL with the American 13 colonies flag and Union Jack sharing equal prominence takes on a pre-Revolutionary War aura in this Tredyffrin Township setting on North Valley road. The mill was established by Thomas Jerman in 1710 and restored by Joseph Jeanes in 1859.

BRUSHWOOD STABLES — Carol Atterbury of Hi-Bid Farm, Willistown Township, and Mark Mintzer, Malvern, make a pretty picture riding by the Ben Clovis Annex of Brushwood Stables, on Sugartown Road, in November of 1991. The 1985 Belmont winner, Creme Fraiche, a gelding, is retired at the 215-acre Malvern horse farm owned by Betty Moran.

THE JEFFERSON BANK (left), of Exton, was built
Richard Thomas III, one of the county's distinguish
citizens, for his son in 1795. It was named Whitford H
and was the centerpiece of a handsome gentleman's far
Whitford Lodge (above), an adjacent office buildi
along Rt. 30, was built about 1810. Thomas manag
the Phila. and Lancaster Company for 39 years, overseei
the operation of Lancaster Pike which passed its 200
year in 1992. The Philadelphia to Lancaster road was t
nation's first turnpike. Thomas was a member of the 4t
5th and 6th U.S. Congress and served on the Provinc
Conference June 18, 1776 which appointed Pennsylvan
delegates who signed the Declaration of Independenc
Whitford Hall was always a residence but vacant in rece
years until Jefferson Bank restored it and re-opened i
doors in 1990.

THIS WHITE OAK at London Grove Meeting was alive and growing when William Penn came to Pennsylvania and named Chester County in 1682.

UNIONVILLE POST CARD ALBUM — Meticulously kept homes of the Victorian and Federal architectural vintage, greet the visitor to the main street of Unionville which is Route 82. Wrought iron, white and gray picket fences accent the properties. Barn (bottom right) lies across the street from the Willowdale Country Store.

ROBINHURST a Kennett Square address with a past. Charles Pennock, an ornithologist, and town character, named the Victorian-Federal style building soon after he bought it in 1891. One day he travelled to Philadelphia for a bird club meeting at the Union League and did not return home. The Kennett paper devoted columns to his mysterious disappearance. After a few years, his wife, the former Mary Scarlett, assumed he was dead and gave all of his stuffed birds to the Phila. Academy of Sciences. Then, seven years after he vanished, he was discovered writing about birds in the Florida Everglades. He returned home and reportedly expressed anger over his wife's giving away all of his stuffed birds. The Pennocks, related to baseball great Herb Pennock, were one of five families to live in this beautiful home at Bachelor Alley and N. Union St. built in 1858. Current residents are Betsy and John Scarlett Halsted. He is the borough and county solicitor and grandson of state senator George Bailey Scarlett.

A STUDY IN SYNCHRONIZED STEPS through the early autumn beauty of Chester Springs' Bryn Coed Farm and the Dietrich Estate. This is the Brandywine Driving Society made up of four-in-hands, two horse and one-horse carriages in one of its periodic outings in October, 1990.

WINTER

THERE'S NO CHARM like the pungent smell and the warm look of a log fire in an old inn with the piano playing softly in the background on a snowy night during the Christmas season. All of those components come together in these 1989 photographs of the Kimberton Inn (c. 1796). While you dine along the front of the building your view (above) is of the Cricket Corner gift shop across the street.

EVERYTHING'S JUST DUCKY for these three white feathered friends who have taken permanent residence at this Christmas card spring house along Greenhill Road, West Chester.

"LET'S GO FOR A RIDE, MOM" beckons Cotton (right), the poodle, who taps on her mistress' back door at Greenridge Road, Glenmoore. La Quita Della Penna has only to walk across the street to Uwchlan Farm and rope in "Patty" to comply with Cotton's wish.

FOR MORE of Uwchlan Farm, please turn the page.

Uwchlan Heritage

Reg. No.

Born: December 5, 1949
Sire: Bandleader of Brooklawn
Dam: Brooklawn Heritage's Lady

UWCHLAN FARM, pretty enough for a Christmas Tour and old enough (c. 1725) to be fascinating; in fact, the oldest farm house in Uwchlan Township. The earliest settlers were Welsh. Uwchlan — pronounced Yewklin — distinctly a Welsh name, means land above the valley — Great Valley. The McClure family bought the original 315 acres from descendants of William Penn. Since then, 20 families have lived here down to Gary and Roberta Moore, who bought the now 15-acre horse boarding farm complete with horsey historical barn plaques in 1988. Beams in dining room above (1725) are original with plans to expand fireplace to its historical dimensions. Sitting room at right dates to 1789.

HISTORY — There were plenty of Indian trails running through Glenmoore before the Welsh settled there in the early 1700s, and Little Conestoga Road was one of them. Fairview Presbyterian Church (above, fore and aft), established in 1838, anchors the area. Larry and Stephanie Posner's 482 Little Conestoga Road farm (right) was built in 1761. It is believed the house was a former inn for cattle drivers, called Lamb Tavern.

THE GUV SLEPT HERE — Former Pennsylvania governor James Earle was born at Raymond and Antoinette Jewell's Pleasant Hill Plantation (left) 151 Little Conestoga Road. The first section was built in 1750. Isaac Van Leer bought the place in early 1800s. His cousin was Gen. Mad Anthony Wayne, Revolutionary War fame, whose spurs were found under the floor boards in the attic. Dorothy Adams, long time resident, made the discovery.

MORE RELICS — Blessed with great quantities of durable Chester County field stone, the masons of the 1700s built their houses and barns to last. For example, the old stone house leading in to the village of Font (top right), the barn on Styer Road (middle) and the stucco-covered house with attached log cabin (right) on Little Conestoga Road which goes with the stone barn on pages 84-85.

STILL LIFE — Snow and ice storm has these two horses literally frozen in their tracks, one in the barn and one thinking about it along Little Conestoga Road near the Fairview Presbyterian Church in Glenmoore.

PHOENIXVILLE HISTORY — Mansion House (above) is tied in with Lincoln's Gettysburg Address. Two buildings (right) east of town on Rt. 23 were part of William Penn tract and date to 1735 along with their original fireplaces and beehive ovens. **Reeves Mansion** (below) was built by the founder of Phoenix Iron and Steel (c. 1858), was a convent for Catholic nuns in 1959, and in 1992 headquarters for an investment counseling firm. **Mansion House** on Bridge Street was around when Cornwallis crossed the Schuylkill on Gordon's Ford in 1777 enroute to Philadelphia. Wayne McVeigh, son of Major McVeigh who owned the **Mansion House**, accompanied Lincoln in 1859 to dedicate the Gettysburg cemetery where he gave his Gettysburg Address. The connection? McVeigh's mother was a Lincoln and he was at age 26 a top figure in the Pennsylvania Republican Party. He later became attorney general in President Garfield's administration and Ambassador to Italy. He died in 1934 at age 97. Current owner and innkeeper Warren Frock said today's **Mansion House** is a fusion of five buildings. One existed in the 1700s.

DARDON PARK hockey player at work.

EAST LANCASTER AVENUE: (above), Corner of Rt. 113, circa 1815. John Webster House c. 1830 (below).

GEORGE FAIRLAMB House c. 1815.

87

BANKERS ROW in a March 1992 snowstorm — West Chester history is tied up in the strip of banks on a High Street named for its lofty (456 feet) elevation in the borough. The Thomas U. Walter Greek Revival architecture of Fidelity Bank, left and the First National Bank of West Chester (nee 1863) bracket the 13 North High Street building which was built in two sections, 1789 and 1793. The *West Chester Gazette* newspaper was published there in 1794. The first burgess, William Sharples, lived there as did the family of botanist David Townsend who served as first cashier of the National Bank of Chester County which opened there in 1818. Walter designed Fidelity's predecessor bank in 1835. The Bank of Chester County is on the corner of High and Market (insert), formerly Dime Savings. Controversy raged when Dime Savings had the old Turks Head Inn razed in 1964. Turks Head was so old the borough was formerly named after it. Snipers took pot shots at General Howe's troops from its porch during the Revolutionary War.

WEST CHESTER

RESTORED — 302, 304, 310 N. High St.

BUNNY in a March snow storm, 108 S. High St.

BERNICE BALL'S HOUSE — Founder of Chester County Day tours, 20 E. Washington St.

VICTORIAN 526 N. Church across from Barclay Retirement Home.

STREET SCENES

BAPTIST CHURCH of West Chester, S. High St. More Thomas U. Walter influence.

FARMERS & MECHANICS BLDG., tallest building in town, Market & High Sts.

ORE ONION SNOW — 26-28 E. Washington St.

SHOVEL READY — 30 E. Washington St.

ELVERSON

WHERE THE TRAIN RUNS NO MORE — The Elverson Railroad Station (right) was built in 1897, but now it's a real estate office. The trains stopped running there in 1981. Some street scenes from the northwestern town (above) including the old Elverson Hotel, January, 1992.

PARKESBURG LANDMARK — The Victorian Gibson House (c. 1874, top left) catches the eye as one drives south on Rt. 10 about two miles south of Parkesburg. Ray Lockhart restored the place by 1991 and wife Darryl did the interior decorating (center photos) just in time for the Parkesburg Christmas Open House. Their giant schnauzer, Handsome, dressed up for the occasion, complete with antlers. The barn dates to 1860, the rear house (upper right) to the 1700s. It's all part of Crestview Farm.

FILLY WITH A BLAZE — Haarmony, owned by Shelly Temple, makes a pretty picture against backdrop of Wrights Estate (circa 1823) on Wrights Lane, West Chester. Wrights Lane Reservoir is shown at sunset (top) taken from Airport Road. Brian Johnston (left), author's grandson, offers his arm to Haarmony for lunch.

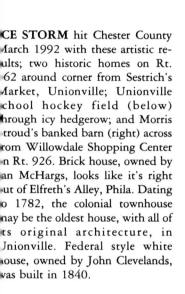

ICE STORM hit Chester County in March 1992 with these artistic results; two historic homes on Rt. 162 around corner from Sestrich's Market, Unionville; Unionville School hockey field (below) through icy hedgerow; and Morris Stroud's banked barn (right) across from Willowdale Shopping Center on Rt. 926. Brick house, owned by Dan McHargs, looks like it's right out of Elfreth's Alley, Phila. Dating to 1782, the colonial townhouse may be the oldest house, with all of its original architecture, in Unionville. Federal style white house, owned by John Clevelands, was built in 1840.

CHRISTMAS CARD — Across from the West Whiteland Park Nature Study area on South Whitford Road is this scene right out of Currier and Ives. The rambling colonial house and the log cabin across the street date to the 1700s.

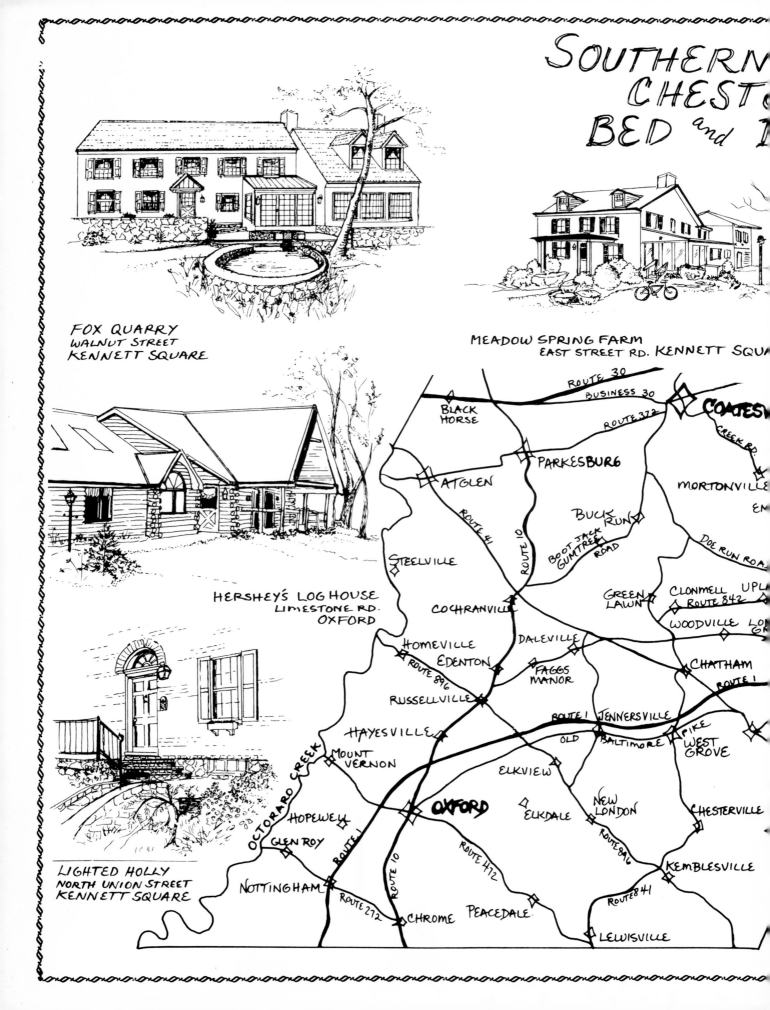

FOX QUARRY
WALNUT STREET
KENNETT SQUARE

MEADOW SPRING FARM
EAST STREET RD. KENNETT SQUA

HERSHEY'S LOG HOUSE
LIMESTONE RD.
OXFORD

LIGHTED HOLLY
NORTH UNION STREET
KENNETT SQUARE

ROUTE 30
BUSINESS 30
COATES
ROUTE 372
CREEK RD.
BLACK HORSE
PARKESBURG
ATGLEN
MORTONVILLE
EM
BUCK RUN
ROUTE 41
ROUTE 10
BOOT JACK GUMTREE ROAD
DOE RUN ROA
STEELVILLE
GREEN LAWN
CLONMELL UPL
ROUTE 842
WOODVILLE LO
CO
COCHRANVILLE
DALEVILLE
HOMEVILLE
EDENTON
ROUTE 896
FAGGS MANOR
CHATHAM
ROUTE 1
RUSSELLVILLE
ROUTE 1 JENNERSVILLE
HAYESVILLE
OLD BALTIMORE PIKE
WEST GROVE
MOUNT VERNON
ELKVIEW
OCTORARO CREEK
OXFORD
ELKDALE
NEW LONDON
CHESTERVILLE
HOPEWELL
ROUTE 1
ROUTE 10
ROUTE 472
ROUTE 896
GLEN ROY
NOTTINGHAM
ROUTE 272
CHROME
PEACEDALE
ROUTE 841
KEMBLESVILLE
LEWISVILLE